**NEW VIC THEATRE**

The New Vic Theatre, Newcastle-under-Lyme presents

# Smoke
## by Bryony Lavery

*Smoke* was first performed on 17 February 2006 at the New Vic Theatre, Newcastle-under-Lyme.

## Smoking, Stalking and Haunting …

"Smoke" is about stalking, haunting and having an excuse for smoking.

Stalking. I have never been stalked, thank goodness, but the beginning of the play, when Rod turns up at Donna's door and asks her out, did happen to me. I turned my man down, but as I continued varnishing my kitchen floor (you see how Life imitates Art?) I did work out this "what if" stalking scenario. And sure enough, he did persist in pursuing me, just a bit, just a bit too much, but not in any way that would make a good play!

Haunting. That is supernatural stalking, isn't it? Here are my haunting experiences. Until I was 11, my family lived in a haunted house. We had one room, down a long passage, in which none of us were keen to sleep. In the middle of the night the dark shape of a little old lady would bend over the bed. Then there's the terrible church somewhere in Wales I visited with a group of actors. We had heard it was haunted, so we set out laughing and joking ready to have a jolly time being frightened … I have a photograph of us all outside the church before the visit … cheery smiles, pink cheeks … then we went into the church … I have the photograph of afterwards … no smiles, white faces … and then there was the flat in Venice where I somehow didn't dare go to sleep … and there was a dreadful stench in one spot that we just couldn't make fragrant … Before you think I am Derek Acorah in female form … these things happen rarely with me.

Smoking. When I wrote this play I was still a smoker and smokers write characters who smoke. I apologise profoundly to the unfortunate actress who has to choke and cough her way through the part of Donna! Those following the Art Imitating Life theory will be interested to hear that the characters in the play I am currently writing don't smoke at all, but like drink just a *little* too much.

Bryony Lavery
**January 2006**

# Smoke
## by Bryony Lavery

## Cast

| | |
|---|---|
| Robert Cameron | Rod |
| Sally Carman | Donna |
| Michael Hugo | Tom |
| Lisa Millett | Theresa |

## Creative Team

| | |
|---|---|
| Director | Gwenda Hughes |
| Designer | Jess Curtis |
| Lighting Designer | Daniella Beattie |
| Music & Sound Design | James Earls-Davis |
| Fight Director | Kate Waters |
| Company Stage Manager | Andy Billington |
| Deputy Stage Manager | Sue Yeomans |
| Assistant Stage Manager | Imogen Ensoll |
| Stage Management Trainee | Steve Hall |

Set and props made by the New Vic workshop.

Costumes by the New Vic costume department.

Lighting and sound operated by Daniella Beattie, Andy Kimberley, James Earls-Davis and Peter Morgan.

Music played by James Earls-Davis and Russell Gregory.

Projection photography by Tim Vickerstaff

New Vic Theatre, Etruria Road, Newcastle-under-Lyme, Staffordshire, ST5 0JG   www.newvictheatre.org.uk

## The New Vic Theatre

The Victoria Theatre Company was the first professional company in Britain to perform permanently in the round - that is, with the audience on all sides of the acting area. Today, the New Vic is known both for its professional productions and for its award-winning work in the community.

The company's origins go back to the late Stephen Joseph, director, actor, designer, lecturer and writer. In the late 1950's, along with other younger theatre practitioners, he was ambitious to renew the vitality of British theatre, founding the Studio Theatre Company to explore a new layout for performance: theatre-in-the-round.

The company's first base was Scarborough from which it toured the country taking the 'theatre' with it - raked platforms providing in-the-round seating for 250. Newcastle-under-Lyme was visited regularly and a permanent North Staffordshire home was planned. On 9 October 1962, a converted cinema opened its doors as a theatre, an event that received no mention in the national press. The company moved to a new, purpose-built theatre, The New Vic, in 1986.

Under the leadership of founding Director, Peter Cheeseman, the company became known for documentary drama with productions such as *The Fight For Shelton Bar* and *Jolly Potters* reflecting the preoccupations of and the issues affecting the communities of North Staffordshire, with its economy based on ceramics, coal and steel.

In 1998, Peter Cheeseman was succeeded as Artistic Director by Gwenda Hughes who has worked extensively in British theatre as an actor and director. For ten years, she was Associate Director with Birmingham Rep and has directed award-winning work in London's West End. Following her appointment, the New Vic has adopted an increasingly outward-looking and collaborative approach to the communities it serves, seeking to re-define the ways a theatre can contribute to the cultural, educational, social, recreational and economic lives of the communities it serves.

Next Step Borderlines project, 2003. Photo: The Sentinel

This has led to the setting up of an Education Department to work within formal education, and the company's ground-breaking outreach department, New Vic Borderlines, which concentrates on work that encourages, enables and promotes Social Inclusion, Community Cohesion and Neighbourhood Renewal. Today, the Education and Borderlines departments are responsible for one third of the company's work.

Central to the company's ethos is the belief that each aspect of its work is of equal value. The language of 'audiences' has given way to one of 'engagement'. A young person devising a piece of theatre with Borderlines, the audience for a Shakespeare play, or a class of primary school children working on reading skills are all engaged with the New Vic and all are of equal importance.

Siswe Banzi Is Dead, 2005  Photo: Robert Day

Once We Were Mothers, 2004. Photo: Robert Day

The New Vic continues to address issues of concern to people locally. It believes in the power of theatre to change lives for the better. It believes that everyone has creative and artistic abilities and that, through encouragement, participation and example, they can be enabled to fulfil their creative potential.

Two Days As A Tiger, TIE project, 2003. Photo: The Sentinel

The Marriage of Figaro, 2002. Photo: Robert Day

The New Vic Theatre operates thanks to a unique partnership between Arts Council England, Staffordshire County Council, Newcastle-under-Lyme Borough Council and Stoke-on-Trent City Council

Charity Number 253242

## The Stephen Joseph Theatre, Scarborough

**STEPHEN JOSEPH THEATRE SCARBOROUGH**

Following its New Vic run, *Smoke* goes to the Stephen Joseph Theatre, Scarborough, the New Vic's 'sister' theatre.

The SJT, the UK's first theatre in the round, has just celebrated its 50th anniversary year. It was in 1955 that theatrical pioneer Stephen Joseph brought the radical idea of theatre in the round from America to Scarborough.

50 years on and the SJT is still going strong under the Artistic Direction of Alan Ayckbourn, who is one of this country's most performed living playwrights. The SJT has produced almost all of his plays as well as commissioning and producing new work by a wide range of writers.

Throughout its history the SJT has regularly originated work which has gone on to be seen in London's West End, at the National Theatre, on Broadway and around the world. Its national and international inflence attracts theatregoers from around the world.

# The Company

## The Cast

### Robert Cameron - Rod

For the New Vic: *As You Like It.*
Theatre includes: *Diana of Dobsons, The Taming of the Shrew, Fiddler on the Roof* (West Yorkshire Playhouse); *Death of a Salesman* (Compass, UK Tour); *King Lear, Love at First, A Christmas Carol* (UK Tour); Bryony Lavery's *Precious Bane* (UK Tour) and *Dracula* (UK Tour). Television includes: *Eastenders: Ricky & Bianca; Heartbeat, Keen Eddie, Holby City, The Basil Brush Show, Shane, Where The Heart Is, 24 Hour Quiz.* Robert has also directed *Love at First* (Edinburgh) and *The Ribbon Cage* (RADA). Robert trained at The Webber Douglas Academy and The University of Birmingham.

### Sally Carman - Donna

At the New Vic (with Northern Broadsides): *School for Scandal.*
Theatre includes: *Antigone, Poetry or Bust* (national tours for Northern Broadsides); *Once Upon a Time in Wigan* (Tour for Urban Expansions); *Thick as a Brick, Big Trouble in Little Bedroom* (Hull Truck); *TV Tots* (Riverside Studios); *Lighting the Day* (Magowan Theatre); *Salford Stuffers* (North West Playwrights). Television includes: *Shameless* (Series 2 & 3 for Company Pictures); *Holby City, Trail of Guilt, Doctors, 4x4, City Central* (BBC); *A is for Acid, The Quest, At Home with the Braithwaites* (Yorkshire Television); *Linda Green* (Red Productions); *Bomber* (Zenith North). Radio includes: *Watcher in the Rye* (BBC Radio 4). Sally trained at LAMDA.

### Michael Hugo - Tom

For the New Vic: *A Christmas Carol, Pinocchio, Kes.*
Theatre includes: *Babes In The Wood, The Rise And Fall Of Little Voice* (Coliseum Theatre, Oldham); *Breaking The Code* (Chester Gateway); *Widows* (The Arden Theatre, Manchester). Television & Film includes: *Ideal, I'm With Stupid* (BBC); *Sir Gadabout* (CITV); *The Collector* (Good Guys Films); *A Right Charlie* (MMU Films). Michael trained at The Arden School of Theatre, Manchester.

### Lisa Millett - Theresa

For the New Vic: *A Midsummer Night's Dream, A Christmas Carol.*
Theatre includes: *Wannabe; The Welcome Party, Night Collar, Fall From Grace* (Liverpool Everyman); *Cabaret* (Liverpool Neptune); *Gregory's Girl* (Oldham Coliseum). Television includes: *Vincent, Blue Murder, Cold Feet, Hillsborough* (Granada); *Life on Mars* (Kudos/BBC); *Bodies* (Hat Trick/BBC); *The Virgin Queen, Casualty, Blackpool, The Secret, When I Was Twelve, Judge John Deed,* (BBC); *Big Dippers* (Red Productions); *No Angels* (2 series for World Productions); *Early Doors* (2 series for Ovation/BBC); *In Denial of Murder* (Hat Trick); *Clocking Off* (2 series for Red Productions/BBC); *Flesh & Blood* (BBC/Red Productions); *Kid in the Corner* (Tiger Aspect); *The Cops* (World Productions/BBC); *Where The Heart Is* (Anglia). Film includes: *The Blue Tower* (Monkey in Heaven Films); *Mischief Night* (Mischief Night Ltd); *Millions* (Mission Pictures); *Married to Malcolm* (Ugly Bug Productions) *Under The Skin* (BFI/Strange Dog). Lisa trained at the University of Liverpool.

## Creative Team

### Bryony Lavery - Writer

Bryony Lavery's plays include *Last Easter, A Wedding Story, Her Aching Heart, Flight and Bag;* and adaptations of *Behind the Scenes at the Museum* and *The Magic Toyshop.* Her most celebrated work, *Frozen,* which opened first at Birmingham Rep, then at the Royal National Theatre in July 2002, staring Anita Dobson, Josie Lawrence and Tom Georgeson, was a dark tale of a killer and his victim's mother. It was nominated for a Tony Award and won the TMA Best New Play Award and the Eileen Anderson Central Television Award for Best Play. She is an Honorary Doctor of Arts at De Montfort University. Future work includes Angela Carter's *Wise Children* for the Royal National Theatre, *The Thing With Feathers* for the McCarter Theatre, Princeton, USA and *Dirt* for Manhattan Theatre Club.

### Gwenda Hughes - Director

For The New Vic: *A Christmas Carol, East Lynne, Dancing At Lughnasa, Pinocchio, Once We Were Mothers, A Woman Of No Importance, Four Nights*

In Knaresborough, Kes, Hector's House, The Beauty Queen Of Leenane, Romeo And Juliet, By Jeeves, Toad Of Toad Hall, Big Maggie, Who's Afraid Of Virginia Woolf?, Moll Flanders, The Wizard Of Oz, Office Suite, Broken Glass, She Knows You Know!, Othello, A Passionate Woman, The Tenant Of Wildfell Hall. Theatre: as Associate Director of Birmingham Rep over twenty-five productions including: Whispers Of Angels Wings, Landslide, The Winslow Boy, Nothing Compares To You, Loot, Entertaining Mr Sloane, Once On This Island (also West End and Olivier Award for Best Musical), Translations, Noises Off and Hobson's Choice; over fifty productions for children at Theatre Centre and for Watford Palace TIE. Gwenda has worked as a freelance director with Perspectives Theatre Company, Unicorn, M6, Red Ladder, Women's Theatre Group, The Young Vic, Oldham Coliseum, Lip Service, the National Youth Theatre and Salisbury Playhouse.

### Jess Curtis - Designer

For The New Vic: As You Like It, Once We Were Mothers, To Kill A Mockingbird, Once A Catholic, The Duchess of Malfi, Blue Remembered Hills, Second From Last in the Sack Race. Theatre includes: Cinderella (Oxford Playhouse); Twelfth Night (Regent's Park Open Air Theatre); Rhapsody (The Royal Ballet); Rookery Nook (Oxford Stage Company); Soap, Fields of Gold (Stephen Joseph Theatre); A Winter's Tale (National Theatre Studio); Hysteria, The Rise And Fall Of Little Voice, Relative Values (Salisbury Playhouse); Mean Tears, Kick For Touch, Small Change, Friendly Fire (Sheffield Crucible); The Wizard of Oz (West Yorkshire Playhouse); Dangerous Corner (Garrick Theatre, London); The Rake's Progress, Don Giovanni (Royal Scottish Academy of Music and Drama, Glasgow); Macbeth, Orpheus In The Underworld, Bastienne and Bastienne (Denmark); Clandestine Marriage, Dreams From A Summerhouse (Watermill Theatre, Bangor); Arms And The Man (Mercury Theatre, Colchester); Opera Triple Bill (Guildhall School of Music and Drama); Local Boy (Hampstead Theatre/Tour).

### Daniella Beattie - Lighting Designer

For The New Vic: A Christmas Carol, Sizwe Banzi Is Dead, As You Like It, East Lynne, The Graduate, Kitty And Kate, Pinocchio, To Kill A Mockingbird, Once We Were Mothers, Can't Pay Won't Pay, Amadeus, Beauty & The Beast, Kes, Carmen, Once A Catholic, The Lonesome West, Love Me Slender,

The Duchess Of Malfi, The Marriage of Figaro, Outside Edge, The Beauty Queen Of Leenane, Pump Boys And Dinettes, Romeo And Juliet, Billy Liar, All That Trouble That We Had, For New Vic Borderlines and Education: Our Country's Good, Blow The Whistle, Lost, The Caucasian Chalk Circle, The Ash Girl, A Midsummer Night's Dream, Home From The Past. Other theatre includes: The Mikado (The Orange Tree, Richmond).

## James Earls-Davis - Sound Designer

For The New Vic: all main house Sound Designs since 1987 including A Christmas Carol, Sizwe Banzi Is Dead, As You Like It, Four Nights In Knaresborough, The Lonesome West, The Duchess Of Malfi, Sweeney Todd, The Beauty Queen Of Leenane. Original Music includes: Once We Were Mothers, Kes, All That Trouble That We Had (all with Russell Gregory); Misery, Dealer's Choice, Romeo And Juliet (2001 with Sue Moffat), Romeo And Juliet (1996), Broken Glass, Antigone, Our Country's Good, (with Russell Gregory). Sound Design/Original Music Includes: Homefront, Sticks And Stones (Reveal Theatre Co); Twelfth Night (Belgrade, Coventry); Her Big Chance (Harrogate); soundtracks for the films On A Hiding To Nothing, A Good Earner?, Taken Without Consent, Dead Ball (with Russell Gregory & Ian Bayliss) (Acting Out Company).

## Kate Waters - Fight Director

Kate is one of only two women on the Equity register of fight directors. For the New Vic: Beauty & The Beast, To Kill A Mockingbird, Four Knights in Knaresborough, Kes . Theatre includes: A View From The Bridge (Bolton Octagon); The Wind In The Willows, Les Liaisons Dangereuses, Playhouse Creatures, Dead Funny (Theatre by the Lake, Keswick); Romeo & Juliet, Nelson, Cyrano de Bergerac, Our Country's Good, Mary Stuart (Nuffield Theatre, Southampton); The Children of the Crown (Nottingham Playhouse); The Ladykillers, As You Like It, Private Lives, The Comedy Of Errors (Northcott Theatre, Exeter); Lonestar Mark Three (Salisbury Playhouse); Canterbury Tales, Blue Remembered Hills (Dukes, Lancaster); seven productions for Shakespeare @ The Tobacco Factory (Bristol) including Macbeth and The Changeling; Romeo & Juliet (Creation Theatre, Oxford); Kes (Royal Exchange, Manchester); Little Women (Duchess, London West End); SpeakEasy, The Servant of Two Masters, Amazing Grace (for Michael Bogdanov); The Rover (The Royal Welsh College of Music & Drama).

# The New Vic Company

# Bryony Lavery

# Smoke

ff

*faber and faber*

First published in 2006
by Faber and Faber Limited
3 Queen Square, London WC1N 3AU

Typeset by Country Setting, Kingsdown, Kent CT14 8ES
Printed in England by Mackays of Chatham plc, Chatham, Kent

A CIP record for this book
is available from the British Library

ISBN 0–571–23348–1
978-0–571–23348–9

2 4 6 8 10 9 7 5 3 1

## Author's Note

The odd line lengths
weird          spacing
and plethora of exclamation marks
and question marks in the text
are the author's attempt to convey
the frenetic nature of these characters
in their situation!!!

/ in the text indicates one character
talking over another

# Characters

*in order of appearance*

**Donna**
a young woman

**Rod**
a young man

**Theresa**
a young woman

**Tom**
a piece of charred ectoplasm

*Time*
the present

*Place*
a small town somewhere

# SMOKE

# Act One

*Blackness.*
  *We are somewhere familiar, resting in a vast darkness.*
  *Something like smoke lingers . . .*
  *A small red glow. Someone is smoking. It is . . .*

## ONE: RESOLUTE

*Donna, a modern woman, resentful of a God stupid*
*enough to put calories in the most delicious food . . .*
  *She is alone and without clutter.*
  *Of her world, there is only heat, cold, light, sound,*
*smell, touch, taste and the bare minimum of recognisable*
*ordinary objects, which arrive and depart, appear and*
*disappear as required.*

**Donna**
  Smoke . . . ?????
  When this started?
  No way Ho-zay.

*She puts out the cigarette . . .*

  Health Regime.
  Five helpings vegetables fruit
  steamed green crap.
  Muesli.
  Dancercise. Lane swimming.
  Chilates. FitBall. Choosing to walk.
  Get Off That Bus one stop before Yours.
  Go That Extra Mile.
  I was turning it all around.

One litre of sodding water *every* day.
*No* Coffee! *Fruit* tea!
Really turning over a new leaf.
Making a Life Choice for a Better
Fitter Slimmer Me
you know?

Then
one evening

(for my dinner
I've had three rice cakes
with a scraping of hummus
only *two and a half points* Weightwatchers
Eat-What-You-Want!!! The way to
that slimmer You . . . )

and

I've done my affirmations three times
bathroom mirror
looking directly into my own eyes

'I will never ever accept anything less
than the love I deserve'

and

I'm clear-varnishing my kitchen floor
Going for a *clean* look throughout the flat.
Feng Shui celestial sweeping.
'86 the Clutter Both In Your Home
and in Your Personal Life'
Changing Rooms.
Makeover.
'Clear the Air in your Accommodation Areas for
Those New Opportunities'
to . . .
Make Space
Space

The Final Frontier
Boldly Go

door bell

*Door bell rings.*

I'm *so* not dressed .
make-up? As *if*!!!!

*Door creaks open somewhere . . .*

Shadow falls

*A shadow falls.*

it's this          guy
I don't know him

Yes?

*Rod, a man in his thirties, materialises . . .*

**Rod**
  I've just been
  I've just finished loading up the van
  my van
  across the road
  the factory
  I wondered
  if you'd
  d'you fancy
  d'you want to come have a drink
  with
  I'm just
  pub
  a drink
  with me?

**Donna**
  Oh.
  Well.

I'm just clear-varnishing my kitchen floor
So /
But
I can't anyway.

**Rod**
I work / at the factory across the . . .

**Donna**
Oh!
Right!
Central Heating . . .

**Rod**
Components /
And I was just

**Donna**
I'm clear-varnishing my

**Rod**
Oh!

**Donna**
So I can't really

**Rod**
Right!

**Donna**
*So*

*An awkward pause . . .*

**Rod**
Just thought I'd . . . (*ask*)

**Donna**
But

**Rod**
*So*

**Donna**
　　Kitchen floor!

**Rod**
　　Got you!

**Donna**
　　But

**Rod**
　　Only I've seen you
　　Off and on

**Donna**
　　Right! Have you
　　Thank you for asking though

**Rod**
　　Thought I'd ask

**Donna**
　　No harm in asking!

**Rod**
　　Well, that's what I figured . . .

**Donna**
　　But kitchen floor!!!

**Rod**
　　Got you!
　　Another time

**Donna**
　　Yes

　　*He disappears.*

　　'*In Your Dreams?*' I think.
　　Yet.
　　I'm a bit flattered.
　　Looking Good, Kid

From Waaaaay Across the Street!
Getting Offers
Approaches.
The Feng Shui      kicking in
Celestial Clearing making that
Happening Thing      happen
Affirmations     right back atcha!
except I'd prefer someone a bit more . . .

*Physically expresses 'bling'.*

a bit more

*Physically expresses 'oomph'.*

someone who      ticks a few more boxes

I don't think any more about it
until Theresa gets back from Tenerife . . .


## TWO: A HOT WIND

*Theresa, a modern woman for whom the cup of life is always at least half-full . . . of Tequila . . . explodes into the space.*

**Theresa**
  . . . Playa de los Americanos!
What a brilliant place!
Me and Kulvinder just slept while midday
then afternoons we worked on our tans
      siesta
then *Major* Beauty Preparation
cos Kid at *our* age!
Then dinner just stomachliningyouknow
then the Main Street is just bars and clubs
and get this      Wall-To-Wall-Willy!
We decided to just have snogs first few days

because Kulvinder says we don't want folk
thinking we're slags and that way we can
so-to-say Window-Shop for summat
*worth* dropping our knickers for . . .
this is for you . . .

*Hands her a bottle of . . .*

**Donna**
Baileys

**Theresa**
I thought you'd never ask!!!

*Both laugh, short and sharp . . . a kind of 'in-group'
laugh.*

Double over crushed ice
Okay . . . in anything anyhow . . .
So first week we snogged two waiters
from Los Cristianos
then two Brummies mine was a *student*
about nineteen Donna Swear To God!
Kulvinder snogged this married man
from Keighley whose wife was
in the shade with sunstroke

**Both**
Just like in *Magaluf*!!!!!

*They both laugh . . .*

**Theresa**
and one afternoon on the beach
when we'd had cocktails early again
at the beach cabana . . .
I snogged this lifeguard who'd just
come off duty . . .
snogged and

okay    tit work
okay    quite heavy tit work actually

Kulvinder said
'You're going to have to go behind sunbeds
or you're so going to get arrested, kid,
Catholic country hello?' but anyway
his fiancée turned up

**Donna**
Kulvinder's got like standards . . .

**Theresa**
until you've got something she likes!
then it's 'Thank You Very Much'

**Donna**
Oh she didn't

**Theresa**
She sodding did Donna!
This *fit* guy who cleaned out the pool . . .
One-Carlos . . . me and him getting seriously
friendly, she's like 'Loser Hello?'
really clicking . . . she's like 'Minger Whatever' . . .
until the filter gets clogged
and One-Carlos strips down to his swimmies
and then she's like (*imaginary shades on*)
'Fetch me a pina colada,
Theresa, I'm going in at the Deep End!'

**Donna**
Oh, Theresa, it is it's Magaluf all over again . . .

**Both**
that ice cream man in!

**Theresa**
I said
'I'll be civil as we're sharing a room, Kulvinder,
but I've lost all Respect,
she's like 'I'm Sooo Upset . . . (*Fake crying.*)
Not!!!'

**Donna**
She's like . . . a sodding bitch

**Theresa**
'and I can't say I'll
ever be able to forgive you
because there's something about him
that says He Might Be The One!'

*They both drink a large slug of Baileys.*

Then I meet Barry

*A photograph from Theresa's heart to Donna's hands.*

**Donna**
This is . . .

**Theresa**
our holiday rep
this has got to be *so* hushhush, Donna . . .
because liaisons reps slash punter-wise . . .
are strictly . . . *strictly* verboten

**Donna**
Barry

**Theresa**
Green
His *winter* base is Kettering
so distance-wise it's not out of the ballpark . . .

**Donna**
Theresa . . . you can't . . . if you marry him . . .

**Theresa**
What you talking about?

**Donna**
You'll be Mrs . . .

*Then Theresa gets it.*

**Both**
Theresa Green!!!!

*The stereo laugh again.*

**Theresa**
Well        we'll see        early days
he gets leave in October
we might hook up for an early Christmas
he's got a Lanzarote upgrade . . .
whaddya think?

**Donna**
he looks        fun

*Hands back the photograph.*

**Theresa**
That was 'Fantasy Lover' Night.
He's dressed as . . .

(*Puzzled.*) Bruce Forsyth on *Strictly Come*

**Both**
. . . Bond. James Bond.

**Donna**
Right . . .

**Theresa** (*fond*)
Yeah.
I was Shaken And Stirred!

*Stereo laughs.*

Kid, we *So* clicked . . .
and he's *age-appropriate* . . .
and in bed we're compatible because
he agrees foreplay is important
*and*, he goes *Down There*! (*Mimed.*)
and! . . .
he shags like a sodding *train* . . .
And!

I think he might be The One, Donna . . .
I really do . . .
but anyway enough about me
what about me?

*The laugh.*

No, kid, just kidding . . .
what about you?
Oooh . . . check it out . . . Kulvinder sent a message

**Donna**
Yeah?

**Theresa**
'Donna has yer fanny still got cobwebs
on it . . . ?'

*Theresa laughs the short sharp laugh alone as . . .*

Well, has it?

Any action since . . . God? . . . *Kenny*????

**Donna**
And I just came out with . . .

*To Theresa.*

Actually . . .
I met this guy who asked me out . . .

*To audience.*

I do the whole factory-over-the-road
clear-varnishing-the-kitchen-floor-
knock-at-the-door Thing . . .

*To Theresa.*

Yeah!

*To audience.*

and I give it . . . 'She - varnish brush.

He - Factory Opposite Hunk'

But with more

(*Bling!*)

And

(*Oomph!*)

and she's . . .

**Theresa**
Factory?

*To the window . . . glasses on . . .*

this factory?
your factory?
can we see him?
is he one of them?
is it that one in shorts?
tell me it's not that one in shorts, Donna!

**Donna**
And I suppose
circumstances and all that
I bigged him up
made it look like he ticked a lot of boxes
Future-prospects-wise . . .

**Theresa**
He sounds like he's got
shagability, kid . . .
you got any more ice only I think
On the strength of 'the Breaking News'
we need to get *seriously* Baileyed!

*Theresa heads off for ice . . .*

**Donna**
So next time
I run into him in Londis when

I'm getting my allotted chocolate
Weight-Watchers
(*She mimes apostrophe.*) 'naughty day'.
He's like

*Rod materialises . . .*

**Rod**
Hi

**Donna**
and I'm like (*available*)
Hi yourself!

**Donna**
and he's like

**Rod**
finished your kitchen floor?

**Donna**
and I'm like '*Yeah*'
and Positive Affirming Eye Contact
so he's like . . .

**Rod**
so do you fancy . . .

**Donna**
and I'm like
yeah, alright

**Rod**
I know what . . . a / pub meal?

**Donna**
You know what . . . a pub meal . . .
Great!

**Rod**
I know *just* the place . . .
The Eagle and Child?

**Donna**
Terrific!

*To audience.*

The Eagle and Child . . . ????

**Rod**
Friday say . . . eightish?

**Donna**
Terrific!

*They both head off, both pausing at an exit to . . .*

**Donna**
something      *glittery*!

**Rod**
neat upbeat      but casual!!!

*Exeunt.*


### THREE: COMMUNICATIONS

**Theresa** (*off, on mobile phone*)
Hello? Yeah . . .
is that Hotel Miramar . . . ????
*Miramar* . . .
*Hotel*

*Sound of a number of door locks being unlocked.*
  *Theresa enters her own flat, phoning on mobile.*
  *She carries a carrier bag from Homebase.*

Do you speak English, yeah?
yeah?
could you transfer this call through
to The Sunseekers Holiday Travel Reps
Playa de los Americanos branch, yeah?

Solid.

*Waits, improving the shining hour with taking out sample paint pots.*

**Theresa**  (*off phone*)
Eat My Paint Brush
*Linda Barker!!!*

*On phone.*

Yeah?
yeah?
They're *all* at Meet 'n' Greets????

Well . . . can you transfer us to
the *main* office in Los Cristianos . . .
I wanna contact one of the reps yeah
. . . no, it's not personal!
it's . . .
a leisure-industry operatives thing!!!!
I'm affiliated to Sunseekers through a
ClubMed / SolTours tie-in . . .

Grasee-arse.

*To audience.*

Pinocchio.

*Mimes a very long nose suddenly growing . . . then the short sharp laugh . . . then . . . shivers.*

God, it's parky in here!
Polar bloody *Ice Cap*!
Snowy?      where are you?

I thought I left you sitting here . . .

*A very particular spot.*
  *Looks around the room.*
  *Then heads off, looking, slightly disturbed . . .*

(*Off.*) Well, what are you doing
Lying down there . . . ????

*Returns with a huge and adorable white polar bear
cuddly toy.*

I'm sure you were in here, Snowy!
(*but the explanation is . . .* ) 'she's
seriously losing it, campers!!!'
Let's turn up that
Old thermostat again . . .

*She heads off as, into mobile:*

Yeah, I need to contact a Barry Green yeah . . .

It's Theresa. Theresa . . . Brown.

*To audience.*

Oh . . . *What?????*


FOUR: THE EAGLE AND BORED

*Donna and Rod enter, her from the Ladies, him from the
bar, she in glittery top, he neat, upbeat but casual . . .*

**Donna**
And so we're in The Eagle and . . .

*And they are in . . .*
  *A clink of glasses. Donna bored witless. Rod is . . .*

**Rod**
  . . . so while basically packing
and delivering central heating
components isn't really
maximising my potential,
it does keep The Wolf From The Door /

**Donna** (*not encouraging*)
Right

24

**Rod**
I get to use the van, yeah, Big Time
for delivering my candles . . .

**Donna**  (*not encouraging*)
Candles?

**Rod**
Got this candle-making business
little sideline novelty candles you know
fruit heads figures willies skulls
scented aromatherapy

**Donna**  (*not encouraging*)
You make candles

**Rod**
Bigtime.
Once you've done outlay for wax,
moulds, and if you've got the space there's no
rent so overheads are quite minimal just
diesel because, Hello, Van?
Sorted . . . so say coupla
hours a night and like two afternoons
hard graft of a weekend, deliveries what?
two evenings a week, weekends mornings . . .
you're looking at possible profits /of . . .

**Donna**  (*driven to distraction by this, as Rod continues*)
I meant nothing by it.
Nothing.

**Rod**
What, twenty-three, twenty-five per cent /
well, let's just say, say six months, I'll be

**Donna**  (*polite*)
Thanks for a nice evening

**Rod**
able to say

Goodbye to The Day Job
Thank You Very Much!
Profit?
Not Many!

**Donna**
Goodnight

*She kisses him on the lips.*
   *It stops him talking. Silence.*

It was a Crap Snog.

But it was better than listening to him.

*Donna drifts out on . . .*

Work tomorrow (*Fake yawn.*)
Early start (*Fake regret.*)
Beauty Sleep!

   . . . anyway
            see you
                     around . . .

*Exits . . . large relief.*


FIVE: ON THE STREET WHERE YOU LIVE

*Rod touches his lips . . . listening to some wildly romantic music in his head.*

**Rod**
Classic.

Classic.

*Sorted!*

You don't know!

You don't know it's going to happen!

26

You don't know when!
You don't know why!
You don't know Who!
Until it happens!
Then. Bam!!!
Seeing Stars!!!
Flying Without Wings!
It's It!!! Mega!!!!
She's The One!!!
She raises me up . . . so I can stand on mountains . . .
think I've Found Her . . . hey, Get Real, Bro! . . .
I *know* I've Found Her!!!!
Classic!!!
Like it says . . . The Other Half of Me.
My Twin Soul.
Out There
You know . . .
There's A Someone Special for
Everyone.
Think I've found mine . . . Ba Boom!
I know I've found mine.
Bigtime.

*He starts texting on his mobile . . .*

Donna.

R U there . . . ?

I Heart U

*Music swells to fill his head. It is . . .*

(*Singing.*) 'You say it best
when you say nothing at all . . .'

*Theresa on phone, but roaming around with colour pots,
multitasking household jobs dexterously . . .*
   *Snowy attends.*

**Theresa**  (*on phone*)
   Yeah.
   Yeah.
   Yeah.

*Assailed by a dreadful stench in one spot.*

Phhhyerorghhhhh!

*Smells investigatively.*

Bloody disgusting stench!!!!

*To someone on the line.*

   . . . no, Mum . . . not you!
   it's that rotting cabbages smell again!!!!

*Waves her hands about vigorously.*

What?

By this wall . . . Mum . . . same as last time! . . .
No, *not* that one I'm going to knock through
I'm *not* going to knock through . . .
   . . . because *this* wall I'm looking at is
*load*-bearing I think . . .

*Listens. It's irritating . . . Quotes.*

'The high-concept exposed stonework is original to
this listed historic building conversion . . .'

Yes, I *will* get in somebody who . . .
yes
*yes*, Mum!

*Listens. Still irritating . . .*

I'm thinking really upbeat
feelgood colours . . .

*Reads her pot labels.*

'*Marrakesh*'       it's red Mum
'*Damson Crush*'       it's purple Mum
'*Purely Poppy*'       it's pinky-red Mum . . .

*She listens.*

No
No
*No*, Mum!
 . . . Because
I don't like *greens* and *magnolias* . . .

*Listens.*

except in your lounge, Mum, they're *great* in . . .
Yes, well, Anna Ryder Richardson won't be . . .
because it's *not* going to be a *guest* bedroom
that's why!
*Homes and Gardens* says
that's just 99.9 per cent of the time Lost Space
I'm thinking home office I'm thinking
Personal Workout Area I'm thinking
Indoor Planting . . . Ficus . . .
mebbe retro Cheese Plant . . .
Hang on, Mum, I've got Call Waiting . . .
Donna! How *was* it ?
Was it?
Was he?
Oh, how . . .
Did he?????
Oh how . . . Ee-ugh!
Well, dump him.
Yeah.

You can.
Over the phone, pot plant!
Text him, Twat!
No, don't see him again, Jesus!
Look, I'll call you back . . .
I've got my Mum giving me Heavy
Verbal about my . . .
*Leisure Pursuits* room . . . yeah . . .
I don't care *what* pursuits, Donna . . .
just so *she* doesn't factor herself in! . . .
I won't
I won't
I *won't* tell her anything, Donna!
Mum! Sorry!

*Listens.*

Donna.
Well . . . She's pulled this man . . . I know '*About
Bloody Time*!'
only he's a complete tosser so
she's gonna knock him back . . .

*Theresa has moved slightly.*
*A small column of smoke rises . . .*

Christ!

Just a minute, Mum . . .
Oh My God . . . Smoke!!!

*Holds hand out to the smoke . . .*

Freezing!!!

Where's that coming from?

*She moves her hand about, feeling for a draught . . .*

Where the bloody hell is that coming from?
Mum, I have to go . . .

there's *smoke* or sommat in here
I need to sort . . .
Mum . . . I *did* get somebody in!

Survey £567. Hello!

*She's off the phone.*

Sodding Surveyor Missed this!

Tosser!

Did you check that window did you Fanny!!!

*Looks up. Something makes her get Snowy.*
 *Goes. Feels for draughts . . .*

No!

Well, where the bloody hell . . . ?

Oooooh!

*It really is a terrible, terrible, penetrating cold.*

Freezing      *Smoke?????*

*A cold air envelopes her. Lights cross to . . .*


## SEVEN: GOOD MANNERS

*Donna, with a hot, steaming cup of coffee.*

**Donna**
 Theresa says dump him over the phone kid
 but I'm thinking do as you would be done by
 remember how Kenny dumped you Donna
 by just not turning up ever again
 I'm thinking that's Bad Manners
 and Bad Manners is Bad Karma
 and Bad Karma means that what goes round
 goes round look what happened to Kenny!

*Sees we don't know.*

Six months after he dumped me
to *the day*
his business goes belly up
his dad gets done for internet porn
and Kenny gets *shingles* round his groin area!

I shouldn't laugh. (*Does so.*) No. no. be-*have*!

So

'Feel the Fear and Do It Anyway.'
'Breaking down the Wall of Silence.'
'Honesty. A Way Out Of Your Prison.'
They all *advocate* a Hands-On approach.
A say-it-to-their-face type of thing.

I wish I'd just phoned

texted.

*Rod materialises, bunch of flowers . . .*

**Rod**
Hi
These are for you.

**Donna**
Oh. But. Thanks.

**Rod**
D'you like them?

**Donna**
Yeah. Lovely.

**Rod**
No. D'you *really* like them?

**Donna**
. . . Yeah?????

**Rod**

I mean, *really* like them, look?

*Finally she gets that she has to look at them . . .*

**Donna**

Yeah, I *really really* like them . . .

Oh . . .

*There's something in the flowers.*

there's a candle

*She takes it out. Stands it on the table. Shape of a skull.*

**Rod**

It's aromatic. Lavender
For relaxation and harmonising.
Like the shape concept!
Who made it?

*He points with both hands to himself.*

The man!
The man hisself.
Selling *very* steadily all year round . . .
*Flying* off the shelves come Halloween!

**Donna**

Fantastic.
Rod . . .

**Rod**

*You* look fantastic.
Give us a kiss then.

**Donna**

No, listen, no look . . .

*But he's sort of in her face. Its easier to give him a kiss.*

33

**Rod**

Fantastic!

*Points to her coffee.*

**Rod**

You want a muffin with that?
Blueberry muffin?
American-style blueberry muffin-lite???
No? Sure?
Sweet enough?
Go on.

*Bad impersonation from* Father Ted.

Ah go on go on go / on go on!

**Donna**

No.

**Rod**

Ah go on go on go on go on!

**Donna**

*Rod!!!!!*
*Chill!!!!*

*Just . . .*

I have to say

I think we should call it a day.

This isn't working out for me.

I need to move on.

I don't have feelings for you.

It's not working out.
It's all       pear-shaped
It's over.
We're yesterday's newspapers.

I don't want to go out with you.
So. /

Rod.
sorry
okay?

Rod?

**Rod**
Come on, Donna.

Come on, babe?

What's this about?

You got the hump?
What you got the hump about?
This is just a couple thing . . . /
all couples go through rough patches . . .

**Donna**
We're not a . . .

we've only been out . . .

*Lifts one finger . . .*

we're not . . .

There's no point going on . . .

**Rod**
We need to spend quality time together,
babe . . .

do things together

make sweet music, / babe

**Donna**
No, Rod . . . this isn't . . .

**Rod**
You know I love you to bits, / babe

**Donna**
No but you can't yet we've only just . . .
and it's been like (*watch*) hardly any / . . .
yeah, but, you see, Rod . . . I . . .

**Rod**
We / can work this out, babe . . .

**Donna**
No, we can't . . . what I'm / trying to say is . . .

**Rod**
Babe, this is just a rough patch . . .

**Donna** (*to audience*)
I mean talk about
'Men are from Mars, Women from Venus'!

(*To Rod.*) I don't think we gell . . .

**Rod**
We're Magic! / Magic!

**Donna** (*to audience*)
Martian! (*To him.*) I think we're on
diverging journeys romance-wise . . .

**Rod**
We click. We cook. We / rock.

**Donna**
Martian!

I can't get through to him
blank         between us         I mean
*Perspex*
it's like we're in two parallel worlds . . .
so I'm like . . .

*She gets up.*

**Donna**
I have to go.

**Rod**
I'll come with you.

**Donna**
No.

**Rod**
I'll call you.

**Donna**
Don't call me.

**Rod**
I'll talk to you later.

**Donna**
No, you won't.
I don't want you to.
It's over.
We're over.

**Rod**
I'll call you.
When you've calmed down.

**Donna**
I am calm. No.

**Rod**
We'll get through this, babe.

**Donna**
No.
No.
No.

*She's away from him.*

Between the caff and my car
there's a phone call.
I go onto voicemail.
I put the key in the ignition . . .

There's a voicemail.
I drive home.
There's three text messages
three voicemails by the time
I'm at my flat.
I go in
ansaphone blinking.
There's four messages
first is him.

**Rod**
Donna

**Donna**
Second

**Rod**
Donna

**Donna**
Third . . .

**Theresa** (*ansaphone*)
Barry's married!
He's bloody married!
I call *Kettering* just to say 'Hi'
get this Voice
'Who shall I say's calling?'
and I'm like
'Who shall I say's answering?'
and this Voice is like 'Norma.
Barry's wife. And you are . . . ?' Oh, Donna!

*Very moist outburst of crying.*

And like a fridge in here!!!!

*Wails a lot.*

And it *smells*!!!!!

*Lots of sniffing, then . . .*

Sod it
Stuff it. Stuff him.
I'll come to terms with it.
Move on . . . so, listen . . .
I'm going out to get bladdered.
Come with!
'Charades Wine Bar'
It's that one with cork walls.
Towler Street. Past Tescos.
Where we started *off*
on Paulette's birthday.
Donna. Be there!

**Donna**

Next three      him . . .

**Rod**

Donna

Donna

Babes

**Donna**

Time from caff to sofa?
Fourteen minutes.
Captain's Log.
Star Date July 14th 2002.
The Nightmare begins.

*It goes darker . . .*

## EIGHT: TROUBLED DREAMS

*Darkness.*
    *In the darkness we hear a sound of chain-links
shifting. Then the chain rushing to its end.*
    *Like a dog running to the end of its chain, trying to
escape.*
    *This happens three times.*

*We smell smoke.*
    *A small eery flame appears.*
    *Hovers.*

*We hear someone moaning in dreadful agony.*

*The flame moves.*
    *It picks out a human form.*
    *It moves over the human form, as if searching it . . .*
    *The flame lights Theresa, just woken from having
passed out drunkenly, not in bed, but at home.*
    *With her, also apparently passed out, Snowy.*

**Theresa**
    Erhhhhh.

    Ah.

    Oh                    God

    Oh please no.

*She looks about carefully. Encounters Snowy.*

    Oh my God what . . . ?????

    Oh it's you!

*She picks up Snowy. Buries her head in his chest. He
smells dreadful.*

    . . . phyeorrrghhh!

You smell like shit!!!!

*Finds her landline phone. Speed-dials.*
    *The flame hovers above her head, as if looking
down on her. On phone:*

Kulvinder . . . ?
How much did you make me drink?
(*Watch.*) It's five forty . . . seven . . . how much?
Ballpark?
Yes
And?
Yes
No, I didn't. Not gin
I can't bear the taste of . . .

*Listens.*

 . . . Oh
In them cocktails
Yes
Then
And . . .
Sambuca???? When?????

*She stands up.*
    *The flame moves to her side.*

*Light dawns.*

Ohhhh.
Did you have the chicken?

*Theresa prowls. The flame prowls after her . . .*

No . . . just . . .
I feel weird I just wondered if that's what . . .

*From somewhere, she finds a Lucozade bottle, drinks
from it as . . .*

No . . . I *made* myself sick.

No, that's *not* bulimia, Kulvinder!
It's not. It's Self-Management, Hello?

Now.

*Some 'Resolve' in the Lucozade.*

Did I leave with that chef what brought our desserts?

Tony. I thought he was really quite . . .

Oh.

Did you.

Did he.

Is he? (*Calls.*) Hi, Tony!!!! . . .
What's he making you for brekkie?

Top.

*Her mobile rings. She looks for it as . . .*

Gotta run, Kulvinder.

*But she is not capable of running . . .*

My mobile's going.

*Landline off. Search for mobile ring. Locates it in her fridge.*

Yeah?

Well you bloody damn rotten lying bloody
married bloody sodding toe-rag!!!

Through the Los Cristianos office
that's how . . . it actually
doesn't matter . . . it's not relevant
*how* I got that sodding
number Barry the sodding point is you're
bloody married innit?
what do you mean?

Explain      'officially separated' Barry . . .

explain      'in name only'

so how come the Los Cristianos office . . .

old number to what . . .

*The flame moves to hover above the bottle in Theresa's hand.*

Oh

oh

oh

did you

do you

*It enters the bottle. The liquid glows with light. The Lucozade starts bubbling . . .*

No, I can't stop thinking about you either . . .

how     *cuddly*     you are

Very soft, very sweet.

course I love you . . .

*The Lucozade bottle explodes.*

Jesus Mary and Joseph!!!!!

*Lights down.*

*A telephone rings. Two rings. Ansaphone clicks on.*
*Donna appears at a doorway, watches it. It is Rod's voice.*

**Rod** (*on ansaphone*)
Hi, it's me.
If you're there, babe, pick up.
pick up, doll.
pick up.

Only I'm pretty sure you're in.

*She backs away from a window view.*

Are you in the bath?

Washing that gorgeous body of yours?

Pick up.
Pick up Babes.
Babes.
Only I really need to touch base with you
about the weekend.
We need to make plans.
I need to run a few things past you.
drive out in the country . . .
pub meal        candlelit goes without saying

Donna . . . ?
Babe?

Or just a quiet night in, DVD, Chinese . . .
Then . . . Sweet Sweet Music yuck yuck yuck????

Or . . . me . . . you . . . sharing . . .
a bath fragranced with neroli
strewn with rose petals
me        a back rub
you        a foot rub

I really think you're there, listening.

*She moves back.*

I know you, darling
I know what you're like.
What are you like?????

Okay. Catch ya. Bye.

*Donna watches as it clicks off. She knows what will happen next . . . Yup . . . redial . . .*

**Rod** (*on phone*)
Hi, it's me.

Or . . . clubbing????
Just a thought.
Text me. /
I could drop by.
I'm gonna be in your area as it goes.

**Donna**
Disappear.
Like smoke.
Vanish.
Puff

*To audience.*

This goes on 24 / 7

I don't know what to do

*She turns down the Ansaphone's volume control.
To audience.*

I don't know what to do

*Her mobile goes. She looks who it is.*

Him. him. him. him. him. him.

Help

Theresa!

## TEN: DEFENCE

*Theresa enters into Donna's space with a large bag of*
*Doritos plus a pot of salsa dip. They circle the space,*
*playing pass the Doritos, zoning in on the salsa dip.*

**Theresa**

. . . you could change your landline number
get digital the same time then I can come
round yours watch Sky Movies Hello?
I thought I might stay over tonight keep
you company cos my cacking kitchen's
Sodding soaked!!! . . .
. . . and I'm thinking new mobile because
you've had it going One-To-One with
him the future's bright the future's Orange . . .

**Donna**

and I'm made of money. Not.

**Theresa**

We could send Big Bobby around like
we did when Darryl was knocking seven
bells out of me!

**Donna**

Now, that's not fair, Trees . . .
Big Bobby's still on probation from . . .

**Theresa**

It's taking friendship too far, isn't it?
I've brought my stuff for work tomorrow yeah? . . .
I should stay, keep you company yeah? . . .
Let's ask Gay Keith in Accounts to pretend
he's your boyfriend he could leave work
wrapped round you walk you to your car
big big snog roving hands . . .

**Donna**

He's gay. Gay Keith.

**Theresa**

But remember him in role-play on Team-Building
Day . . . *brilliant*!!! . . . he could have you against your
car door his hands inside your . . .
It's taking friendship too far, isn't it?
Okay.
Think think think

*Both pace. Dorito/salsa work . . . then . . .*

**Theresa**

Kulvinder!

We just introduce
Stalker-Nasty-Candle-Man / to her . . .

It's a very good, very fun idea . . .

**Donna**

I'm like 'Don't touch him, Kulvinder . . . /
he's mine !!! . . .'

**Theresa**

I'm like . . . 'Donna's really keen on Rod, /
Kulvinder . . . You keep away!!!'

**Donna**

She's like . . . 'Talk to the hand
Cos the Fanny ain't listening!!!'

Cue
Eyelash / Batting

**Theresa**

Cue Tongue Tennis

**Donna**

Then she's like 'Come out the back
for a bit of privacy I really want to

47

really really talk to you get to know
You bigtime . . .' then
Bada Boom

**Theresa**
Bada Bing

**Both**
He's been Kulvindered!!!!!

*Stereo laugh. Then . . .*
    *Satisfied stereo Dorito-eating.*

*Ansaphone clicks.*
    *Both watch it. Donna stands as Theresa turns it to*
*audible . . .*

**Rod** (*on phone*)
Donna?

You there?

Only I'm just outside.

*They both slightly duck.*

Thought I'd pop in.
Kiss you goodnight.

And good morning if you fancy
yuck yuck yuck

only your light's on . . .

*Both duck down.*

Give us a bell, yeah?

on the mobile, babe.

*Ansaphone clicks off.*

**Theresa**
Bloody hell, / kid . . . !!!!

**Donna**

Shhhhhh!!!!!

*They wait, crouched down.*
*Silence.*
*Then . . . a knock at a door.*
*Silence.*
*Then, somewhere else . . . a knock on a window pane.*
*They flinch down even more.*
*Then . . . from another direction . . .*

**Rod**

Donna?

*Another knock, another window.*
*They whisper, holding each other . . .*

**Theresa**

He's *circling*!!!!

Like those dingoes yeah? on *Wildlife Outback*!

*They lie, flat as they can get, on the floor.*
*The knocking continues to circle them.*

**Donna**

Trees . . . let's just try the Gay Keith idea, yeah?

**Theresa**

I'm sleeping here Donna?
I'm right with you kid.

**Donna**

Oh, Theresa!!!!!
Why am I always so unlucky with men?
Is it because I'm a Capricorn?

**Theresa**

No. It's because you're A Twat, kid.

*Rod is at an entry, watching . . .*

**Rod**
Some        oily        *bastard*!!!!
starts it with Donna!
Some work-colleague toe-rag!
I'm in the habit of just keeping an eye open yeah
Make sure she gets to work okay?
Make sure she gets back from . . .
If you're in love with a beautiful woman . . .
really love someone . . .
you watch your back, yeah?
you don't let anybody come near your girl, yeah?
and you'd be crazy not to keep an eye out, yeah?
you'd be *nuts* not to be on the lookout . . .
there's some guys Donna sees at work . . .
I mean . . . I dunno . . . they're crap at
knowing how to behave . . . when somebody's
spoken for . . . yeah . . . don't know the *boundaries*
and *this* one . . .
all over her like a rash!
I mean        *hands*!
and she's too *nice* to say 'Shove it!!!'
To say 'I'm practically engaged!'
'I've got a fiancé!'
but . . . you know . . . a quiet word in the ear . . .
just . . . quite polite . . . but . . . show the iron fist
under the driving glove . . . yeah? . . . 'I know
what you're up to, pal . . . I know what's going
on in here (*head*) . . . so just . . . back off . . . just
back off, pal, yeah . . . ???
Didn't work.

He's like . . . 'I do what I like with who

I like, chum . . .'

I have a little word with Donna

She's like 'I'm very close to Keith, Rod'
I'm like 'I don't want to be heavy, babe . . .
but if you're my woman . . .
you gotta do what it says on the tin . . .
therefore
it's got to stop.

It has got to stop

Or The Puff gets it.'

End of. Sorted.

*Very fair and forgiving . . .*

Women!

*They are very funny and fluffy . . .*

At the end of the day . . . They don't get it!
They        do        not        get it

Hello?

Her bathroom light's gone on!

*He crouches down.*

He crouches down
fading into the shadows
like a shadow hisself
only his hawk-like forensic eyes
catching the light from the silvery moon . . .

*Outside . . .*

## TWELVE: SMOKE AND MIRRORS

*Theresa comes in . . . dressing gown, hair in towel, face-pack, early stages . . . She is singing, singing, somewhat restricted by fast-drying face-pack . . . something complimentary and modern like . . .*

**Theresa**
'I saw your face
In a crowded place . . .

*Carries a cotton bud, stands before a mirror . . .*

You're beautiful
You're beautiful.'

*She shivers.*

*Draught!!!*
'It's True

You're          beautiful

You're          ow . . . beautiful.'

*The pauses in the song are where she is applying the cotton bud to an ear. This distracts her from seeing, in the mirror, looking at her, something that looks like a half-burned mask.*
    *The mask makes a sound . . .*

**Tom**
haaaah

*It sounds like someone trying to get air in a smoke-filled room.*

aaaaaaa . . . ergh . . .

*Theresa, applying cotton buds to her ears in turn, fails to hear the mask.*

**Tom**
haaaaagh . . .

Haaaagh . . . !!!!!

*Theresa looks at the mask.*

**Theresa**
Aaagh!
What *do* you look like, girl?????

*She runs to wash it off*

**Tom**
Haaagh! Haaaghh! *Haaaagh!!!!!*

*The mask bursts into flame with centuries of frustration.*


THIRTEEN: SELF-HELP

*Inside . . . smoking, holding a full ashtray of cigarette stubs . . .*

**Donna**
'I try everything.
Go ex-directory
New mobile server
He just starts coming to the door
knocking
I'm like MI5!!!
Going out at different times.
From different exits of the flats.
Leaving for work completely random timing.
He follows me, work
dancercise shopping taibo winebar he's there
There there there there!!!
I try doing the Spiritual Thing . . .
Burning sage leaves.

Meditating Sending him Positive Affirming
Cosmic Instructions to Take Himself with
Love and without Regret Out of My Life . . .
Somebody . . . Yeah! . . . Marcia . . . gives me
*The Little Book of Spells* . . .
I do the bloody 'Get rid of
unwanted influences' spell . . . some twigs and
an apple and that
burned at midnight, full moon . . .
I get a kit to make an American Indian
smudge stick to send him into the element
of air . . .
Nothing Works!!!!
Nothing nothing nothing nothing!!!
He's            *always there*
I ask
I tell
I shout
I scream
I bloody weep like a bloody baby
I pray!!!

*She prowls up and down, round and round.*

. . . then I go to the Pissing Police!

*Leaves with enormous energy for the police station . . .*


FOURTEEN: SPRAY

*Theresa enters, in one hand a gorgeous-smelling air-freshener spray, in the other a sachet of pot-pourri on a sizeable pottery dish . . .*

**Theresa** (*reads air-freshener*)
  'Citrus blossom . . .
  a refreshing fragrance blending fresh flowers

54

with an invigorating hint of citrus zest . . .'

*She sprays it everywhere, but particularly in the one smelly spot. Reads pot-pourri label.*

'Essence of Nature
contains at least
fifteen varieties of herbs, roses, and pungent
scented woods to turn your home
into a woodland glade . . .'

*She opens the sachet and pours it into the dish . . .*

Now you're talking!

*She places the dish very deliberately on the very cold spot.*
*Tom's face hovers like mist.*

**Tom**
haaagh!!!!

*Theresa sniffs. Sprays her aerosol again.*
*Tom's disfigured-mask face dissolves.*

**Tom**
Haaaaaaaagh!!!!!

*The sound of a chain running again to its length.*
*Theresa stares at Snowy. Sprays Snowy. Snowy does not move.*

**Theresa**
Sorted!

*Exits.*

## FIFTEEN: LOVE TO HATE

*Rod with candle-mould. A large willy shape. He's waiting for it to get completely cold.*

**Rod**

You see . . .
We're now living in a Nanny State!
Where your own business is everybody's
business, yeah?
Time was . . . there's agitation . . .
you just sort it out . . . personal
private . . . now . . . you sodding *sneeze*
the Dibble's pulled you in
interview room
an air of menace which
the man hisself treats with maddening calm . . .
'What you think you're doing, Bro?'
This with plainclothes insolence . . .
The Man Hisself gives them Nothing but . . .
'It's Nothing.
It's Domestic
A man and his girlfriend have a bit of a ruck . . .'

Suddenly . . . the man can't come within 250 yards
of said girlfriend! . . . *You* tell *me* . . .
is that a Police State or is that a Police State?
Can you conduct a relationship at 250 yards!
Can you *buffalo*!!!

*He darts out as Donna crosses space.*

Babe!

**Donna**

You're not supposed to come near me . . .

**Rod**

The police don't get it!

56

**Donna**

250 yards!!!

**Rod**

I love you, woman!

*Donna says nothing.*

**Rod**

You gotta tell them Babe . . .
we can't not meet
you and me
we've got it going on
we're cooking
with Gas!
we're Magic!

We do what it says on the tin!

Like two mighty lions
big cats
caught in the jungle of their passion
Hunters
Lion Kings

*Donna has been watching him.*
*She comes close to him*

**Donna** (*spits*)

Is that love?

*She puts her finger down her throat . . . gags.*

Is this passion?

*She pretends to pee.*

Is this magic?

*She pretends to crap.*

Because that's how I feel about you!
you're crap!

you're vomit!
you're piss!
you make me sick
you make me crap my pants
you make me sick all down my front!
You make me shit myself!!!!!

*To audience.*

*You* tell me
how could I do it different?
How?
How?
How?

*She exits.*
    *Rod looks at us. Very embarrassed.*

**Rod**

You give somebody *everything*!!!

they throw it back in your face!!!!

*He bursts into furious tears, very ashamed that we can see.*

sod

sod

*sod!!!!!*

*Butches up . . .*

And at the end of the day
you're sick as a parrot
you just want bad stuff for them
who's gonna do it for you?
who?
who?
no bloody body that's who!

She's made me look bad

The disrespect!
The things she said!!!!!

And the        *behaviour*!

I think I need to leave her a little message

don't you?

*He takes out a pair of white surgical gloves. Puts them on. Opens the candle mould. Takes out a willy-shaped candle . . .*

She's a bit thoughtless about security

*He opens a window.*

I wouldn't like a girlfriend of mine
to be this careless

*He climbs in.*

but        a slapper
a        *bleeding tart*
well . . .
somebody opens her legs up to
anybody . . .

somebody        no manners
somebody        dirty

*He's standing in Donna's flat.*

deserves everything she gets

*Picks up a magazine,* Cosmopolitan. *Opens it.*

Men        sex
underwear

'the fifty most-guaranteed-to-get-
an-orgasm sex positions . . .'

You got to wonder . . . (*Loyd Grossman*)
'what kind of a trollop lives in a house
like this . . . ?'

He had a job to do,
and time was short
he emptied his mind of everything
but his trained professionalism

*He puts down the willy-candle on the magazine . . .*

He moved like a panther through
the hostile no-man's-land of the
Dark edifice . . .

*Lights down, as . . .*

## SIXTEEN: A MASTER PLAN

*Up on Theresa, in full maquillage . . . lots of bling-bling,
hot to trot, weekend case slightly smaller than an
average-sized semi-detached . . .*

**Theresa**  (*landline*)
Well . . . why can't we meet in Kettering?
Barry . . . if she's not *in* your life any more
she's not gonna . . .

alright

I'm *not* getting cold feet . . .

it's *not* going off the boil, Baz . . .

*To audience.*

Sorry about this.

*To Barry.*

I *do* love you to bits . . .

you're all the world to me . . .
you are
you are
you are

*Pushed into it . . .*

You're my Barry Big-One . . .

*To audience.*

Shut up!

*To Barry.*

So I take the M13 as far as where?
then I come off at Junction . . . ? Yeah
*second* mini-roundabout *first* exit . . .
about *half* a mile . . .
and the Viking Motel is on the left
after a Mobil garage . . .

*Her mobile goes.*

Bazz . . . mobile . . . I'll see you very soon
can't wait! Miss ya! Love ya! CantWaitTo
BeWithYa!

*To next call.*

What?????

*Answers . . .*

Donna, kid . . . I'm just on my way
out the door . . . can it . . . ?

*We hear Donna screaming and screaming and
screaming somewhere . . .*

I'm coming, Donna!
I'm coming!!!!!

*Lights down on Theresa.*

*Then we are with Donna. She is standing in a
darkness lit by many candle flames.*
*Theresa enters with her weekend case, coat, car keys.*
*Lights on to reveal every surface covered with
novelty candles . . . skulls, willies, etc.*

**Theresa**
OH      MY       GOD!!!!

skulls!

fruit

and

. . . is that a . . . (*willy*)?

It's aromatic!!!!

*Smells it.*

It's *ylang-ylang* . . . !!!!

how weird is that?

**Donna**
I can't take it any more.
I don't know how he got in
I don't know when he's gonna get in again . . .

**Theresa**
You got to ring the Old Bill again.

**Donna**
It only keeps him away for like this much time . . . and
then just when I'm feeling Wow Chill! . . . it
Starts again it starts again it starts again!!!!!

**Theresa** (*puts her arms round her*)
You poor
Twat! You poor little twat!

*Surreptitiously checks her watch.*

62

We got to get you out of here . . .

**Donna**

He'll just *follow* me . . . follow me follow me
follow me follow me

**Theresa**

Okay. Okay. Stop with the reverb. (*Thinks.*)
Ding!
Check it.
We're going to swap cars.
You're going to get in mine
and go to my flat.
I'm going to get in yours . . .
and get Mad Candleman to follow me to Kettering . . .

**Donna**

Kettering . . . ?

**Theresa**

I'm meeting Barry!!!!
Lovers' Tryst Thingy, Hello????!!!

*Donna doesn't get it . . .*

I decoy Candle-Man to Kettering . . .
you leg it to mine!
What Do You Win, Caller?
A Whole Weekend Break Completely
Away From The Stalking Thing In An Up-
And-Coming-Recent-Conversion, Hello!

**Donna**

You're such a good friend to me, Theresa . . .

**Theresa**

What are friends for, Twat?

**Donna**

Okay, Problem!
He'll recognise me, Theresa!!!

*Theresa pauses . . .*

**Theresa**
Ding!
We gotta change coats, kid . . .

*They start changing coats.*

**Donna**
It's your . . .

**Theresa**
Karen Millen!
This is almost taking friendship too far, Twat . . .

**Donna**
Oh, Theresa . . .

**Theresa**
Just don't smoke in it!

**Donna**
Oh, Theresa . . .

**Theresa**
It's gonna be alright, kid . . .
you're soon gonna be tucked up at mine
watching *X Factor*

while MadSod's circling
The Kettering area with me! . . .

*She takes Donna's coat.*

I'm going to meet The Love of My Life in . . .

*Sees the label . . . a spasm of horror.*

New Look!!!

**Donna**
Okay, Problem!
Our Hair, Theresa!!!!

**Theresa**

>DING!!!
>Take me to your wardrobe, Cinders!!!

*Theresa drags Donna off as . . .*


### SEVENTEEN: A CAR CHASE

*Rod enters, dangling car keys . . .*

**Rod**

>Surveillance reveals two twats
>in the building . . .
>that filthy twat with the silver Nissan Micra . . .
>and her prozzy friend . . .

>Vermin

>you're never more than six feet from a rat . . .

>how's the fumigation going?

*Another space. Theresa and Donna appear as each other, holding car/door keys. Bad wigs.*

**Donna** (*to audience*)

>No wonder we never pulled at
>Marcia's Tarts and Vicars Party.

**Theresa**

>What was to pull, Twat?
>Okay . . . car keys
>that's ignition that's the boot.

**Donna**

>The ignition's a bit slow
>so twist it hard then plenty of choke . . .

**Theresa** (*house keys*)

>These four are for the front

that's mortice top and bottom, those are
the Yales . . . these are back door and window
Chubbs . . . and those are all internals so . . .
well . . . I go first . . .

*They hug.*

Crudités cheese-dips pizzas
in the fridge-freezer which is not working
so no ice cream . . . Doritos Pringles Twix
Maltesers top cupboard
wine voddie Baileys etc . . .
well you know where, kid . . .
You might need to give it a bit of a spray
When you get in.
Well, I hope you get some rest
I hope I get *none*!

*Both do the stereo laugh.*

I'll see you Sunday! . . .

**Donna**
Have a *great* time with . . .

**Theresa**
*Barry*

**Donna**
*Barry* . . . !!!

**Both**
Fingers Crossed!!!!

*The three of them in their spaces with their car keys.*

**Rod**
She's vacated!
bitch has vacated!
she's switching location!
walk

66

run
don't matter to me I'm
on your tail!
Heat-seeking missile!

**Theresa** (*singing something like . . .*)
'If this ain't love . . .
why do I feel so good?
why do I feel so good?
why do I feel so . . .'
Tank's nearly empty hello!
Thanks, Donna!!!!

**Donna**
The hole
the hole
the hole
Bloody key!
Bloody key
steering lock's on, Theresa!
Thank you very much!
Oh God oh God oh God oh God oh God . . .

*Three cars start up, drive . . .*

**Rod**
Nissan Micra goes past . . .

metallic silver . . .

her bitch friend!

look at her in her tart's tut!

Wig! Slapper!

**Donna**
So now . . .
I get in the car . . .
set off . . .
down Swingler Road . . .

left onto Palmerston Drive . . .
where Palmerston curves . . .
there's a side road . . .
Bempton Road . . .
he's parked there . . .
I go past . . .
I can see him turn the ignition . . .

**Rod**

Here we go!
The aquamarine Mégane Tartmobile!
here we go!

**Theresa**

Oh, it's us in our big red Renault is it?
come on then, Big Boy . . .
tuck in behind me!

**Donna**

Oh, he's following *her*
he's following *her*!

**Rod**

Where's she going?
The A4506?????
Who's she know there?
Who's she meeting there then?

**Theresa**

Get your big red thing
stuck up behind me, Candle Boy!!!
that's right!

**Donna**

I'm on Braintree Drive
on my own
on my own
on my own!!!!!

**Theresa**

That's right, Big Boy . . .
Harder
Faster
Quicker!
We know how you like to do it!

**Rod**

You won't lose me!

**Donna**

You know what's weird . . .
wherever
wherever
*wherever* I go . . .
he's been *there*
in my mirror!
for the first time in months I know definitely
he's not going to be there behind me!

*Sings.*

'Alleluia alleluia
Alleluia alleluia al – lel – uia . . .'

**Theresa**

Oh . . . nearly lost me, didn't you, Pal?
The Big Red Renault nearly went to Retford
then, didn't it?

Keep with me, Coulthard!

**Rod**

She's driving like a *maniac*!

**Theresa**

First junction!

**Rod**

Shite!

**Theresa**
A2309 Ayrton!

**Rod**
Kettering?
What's she doing in Kettering?

**Donna**
Singing wild and free . . .

**Theresa**
Round the mini-roundabout!

**Rod**
Shite!

**Theresa**
Now . . . I'm looking for . . .

**Rod**
Slowing down!!!!

**Theresa**
Mobil garage on the right . . .

Mobil garage on the right!!!!

**Rod**
She's getting petrol!
Right!
She's filling up!

**Theresa**
. . . go straight past the Mobil garage
for half a mile . . .

**Rod**
No she's not!
she's going on . . .

**Donna**
What a drive!
What a drive what a drive what a drive!

*She is holding Theresa's house keys, in Theresa's space.*
  *Snowy is there, sitting.*

**Donna**
  Nobody here but MEEEEEEE!!!!!

*She takes off her wig, as . . .*
  *Meanwhile . . .*

**Theresa**
  Look for the Viking Motel on your
  left . . .
  oh!

**Rod**
  She's turning off
  she's turning off . . .
  what the . . . ?

**Theresa**
  Viking Motel!

**Rod**
  Viking Motel! Motel!

**Theresa**
  Room 506.

**Rod**
  She's meeting someone
  she's

**Theresa**
  Knock knock!
  it's me!!!!

*She exits into the motel room . . .*

**Rod**
  It better not be anybody . . .
  it better not be anybody in here . . .
  Tart!!!!

**Theresa**
Barry Big One!
Love!!!!

**Rod**
You're dead!
You're both dead!!!!

*He exits towards the motel room . . .*


## EIGHTEEN: THE ANTI-SMOKING LOBBY

*Donna is left alone in the space, which is Theresa's flat.*

**Donna**
Oh My God . . . Peace!

*She physically unknots. Stretches.*

Alone At Last!

*It is wonderful.*
    *A stream of cold air rushes silently into the space.*

God, it's so not warm in here!

Christ!

*She turns, looking.*

Central heating hello?

*Donna wanders around, looking for the central
heating switch in the space.*

Wall-op (*the switch*).

*She studies the complicated controls.*
    *Fiddles with the switch.*
    *The sound of chains chinking and shifting begins . . .*

Wall-op.

*The sound as of a dog rushing to the end of its chain.*

God, Theresa, you need to bleed
Your radiators!

*A terrible stench fills the space . . .*

Oh dear me!

*She finds the aerosol. Sprays it liberally.*

Oh my giddy bloody . . .

*Smell still lingers.*

Well, this is a Perfect Excuse for a . . .

*She gets out a cigarette. About to light it . . .*

Oh!

*Takes off Theresa's coat.*
    *Hunts for her lighter. Strikes her lighter.*
    *In the air, there is a terrified sound . . .*

**Tom** (*voice-over*)
Haaagh!!!!!

*Donna stops, listens. The lighter gets hot. She stops.*

**Donna**
Ow!

*Licks her burnt fingers, shaking the lighter to cool off.*

Now get warm!

*She lights the lighter.*

**Tom** (*voice-over*)
Haaagh!

*She lights her cigarette.*

**Tom** (*voice-over*)
Haaaaagh!!!!

*Donna inhales.*
*Exhales smoke.*

**Tom** (*voice-over*)
Haaaaghhaaaagh-haaaaaaagh!!!!!

*Donna picks up the paint pots.*
*Smoke slowly fills the space.*

**Donna**
'Marrakesh'
'Damson Crush'
'Purely Poppy'

*The sound of something agitatedly running its chain*
*length, repeatedly . . .*

Mmmm . . . in this space . . .
You need to go to a tranquil palette . . .

*She finds a colour chart, flips through it, as . . .*

**Tom** (*voice-over*)
Uuuurghhhh!
Uuuuuuuurgh!!!
Uuuuuuurghhhhh!!!!

*Donna smokes on, looking through the more tranquil*
*palette of . . .*

**Donna**
'Warm Jade'
'Wild Fern'
'Herb Garden' . . .

I'm thinking calmer tones in here, Tree . . .

*Regards the wall, smoking reflectively, very near Tom.*

**Tom**
Haaaagh!!!!!

*One of Theresa's cheery choice paint pots splashes an
arc of Purely Poppy across a wall . . .*

**Donna**
Oh my God!!!!!

*With trembling hand, she brings her cigarette to her
lips, inhales.*

**Tom**
Haaaaaaaaaaagh!!!!!

*Little fountains of water spout from the radiators.*

**Donna**
Oh Jesus!!!!!

Ashtray . . .

*She looks around for an ashtray. There is only the
ceramic pot-pourri container . . .*

Ah!

*She tries to tip her gathering ash into it.*

**Tom**
Haaaaghhhhhhhhhhh!!!!

*A sound of someone rushing along their chain.
    Then the potpourri container moves away from her.*

**Donna**
Oh Mary!!!!!

*She moves the pot-pourri dish back to her.
    It stays.
    She goes to put ash in it.*

**Tom**
Haaaaaaaaagh!!!

*It moves.*

**Donna**

Oh Joseph!!!!!

*She's very scared and wary. To audience.*

The very first time
we come round to view
this property . . . I'm like you know what, Theresa,
kid, it's in a *very* old building . . .
She says 'It's a former tallowmaker's.
Its listed.'
I'm like
think maintenance
think deep pockets . . . and I'm
like 'Trees . . . wake-up call . . . it's *cold*!'

*And very frightening.*

**Tom**

Harrgh harrgh

**Donna**

I'm gonna get Theresa one of
those little North American Indian
space-cleansing kits for this
room.

Little present for having me!

Because there's this
seriously dark corner . . .

*She becomes aware of the seriously dark corner . . .*

really really dark

*She takes her lighter.*
 *Chains shift and clink.*

really really smelly . . .

*She takes the air-freshener.*
 *The chains clink and shift more.*

76

I know it's bonkers but
I'll just check it then straight to bed . . .

*Lights her lighter and sprays her aerosol.*
    *Three times there is the sound as of a wild dog*
*running on its chain . . .*

**Tom**
Haaaaghhhhhh

Haaaaaaaagh!!!!!

Haaaaaaaghhhhhhhh!!!!

*On the third rush, Tom, a once-long-ago energetic*
*young man, now a hideously burnt piece of ectoplasm,*
*appears. He is on the ectoplasmic chain which has all*
*these years been round his neck. His face is very close*
*to Donna's face . . .*

**Tom** *and* **Donna**
Aaaaaaaaaaaaaaghhhhhhhh!!!!!

*Donna backs away as far as possible from him.*


NINETEEN: AN UNLUCKY PURSUED WOMAN
BECOMES EVEN UNLUCKIER

*They look at each other, equally frightened.*
    *Tom attempts a smoke-damaged conversation.*

**Tom**
Heeeeelp meeeee . . . Laaaaasssssssss . . .

**Donna**
Noooooooo . . .

**Tom**
Heeeeeeelp meeeeeee . . .

**Donna**
Doctor Bramacharia
You're overdoing
my mood-alterers . . .
Stop.     Stop it.     Chill.

*She takes out a cigarette and lighter.*

**Tom**
Haaaaaagh!     Haaaagh!     Haaaagh!

*He is running up and down his chain.*

No smoooooke

no fiiiiiiiiiiire.

Noooooooooooooo!!!!

Poor Tom
oh poor poor Tom
oh Tom . . .

*This time he pulls so violently he breaks his chain.*

Oooooooooooooooh!!!!!

**Donna**
You . . .

Is it . . . ?

It's . . .

'No Smoking' in here ??????

**Tom**
You caaaaaaan . . .
Hear me . . . ????

**Donna** (*very little voice*)
Yes.
I see you've been chained up . . . ?

**Tom**
You caaaaaaaaan . . .
Seeeeee meeeee . . . ?????

**Donna** (*even smaller voice*)
Yes.
You're       here       aren't you?

**Tom**
You caaaaannnnn . . .
Understaaaaaaaand me . . . ?

**Donna**
Yes.

**Tom**
You've saaaved me . . .

Oooooohhhh

The chain is brokennnnnn!

Youuuuu've saaaaaaaaved me!!!!

**Donna** (*to audience*)
Why does Stuff always happen to me?

I'm a good person!

I give to earthquake appeals!

I buy *The Big Issue*!

I've done stunts for Comic Relief!

I bought a goat!

This is so not fair!

**Tom**
Saaaaaa . . . viour!

**Donna**
Pardon . . . ?

79

**Tom**

You're my Saaaaaa . . . viour . . .

**Donna**

I beg your . . .

**Tom**

You are my Saaaaint.
My missssstresssss.
My Laaaaaady.

**Donna** (*to us*)

Gotta be a Cosmic
Invisible Label on my forehead . . .

*Shows us.*

'UN     LUCK     Y.'

*Tom, after all these centuries, has found an audience.*
*He seizes the spotlight with ectoplasmic gusto.*

**Tom**

I will forget her what led me here!
That . . . orange basket!

*This is an archaic offensive tit-reference.*

That . . . fishhead-seller!

*This is an archaic offensive fanny-reference.*

That . . . pardon me . . . doxy!

*This is the worst archaic insult.*

I was her . . . ever-present serf
her     knight     every night!
her     constant disciple.
She says, 'Oh Tom, you follow me everywhere
follow me here
sit here
I'll buy us both some roast chestnuts

80

I'll be back presently.'
She's never retuuuuuurned!

**Donna**

That's awful . . .

**Tom**

Then her faaaaather appeaaaaaaarrrrs!
With his two best tallow-dippers!!!
'I tooooold you to leave my lass be!!!
Cease        following my lass!!!'
He lifts his oak cudgel!
He brings it down
Whhhhhaaaaaaack!!!

**Donna**

That's why your face is . . . /

**Tom**

As I sink
The dippers catch me!
Put this piece of mischief around my neck.
Are they still here?

**Donna**

I'm not a big expert on . . .

*A mime representing 'ghost / ectoplasm / haunting'.*

**Tom**

The dippers
That pilèd up the straw the kindling
Here here here
Then threw the smouldering rag
'There! Now you're Alight With Love, Lad!!'
And          pfifff!

**Donna**

That's why your side's all . . .

**Tom**

Are they still here????

Or are they in Hell?????

**Donna**

I'm actually not very religious so . . .

**Tom**

I run hither thither (*He shows us.*)
Thither hither (*He shows us.*)
Up this chain (*He shows us.*)
Down this chain.

**Donna**

Whatever he is . . .
He's repetitive . . .

**Tom**

And HER!!!
Is she in Heaven
Or is she in Hell?

**Donna**

Hell. / Gotta be.

**Tom**

I run hither thither
Thither hither
Up this chain
Down this chain

*Tom believes this to be as fascinating as Rod finds the manufacture of candles.*

Hither

Thither

**Donna**

This goes on       all night
It's like       I've freed him . . .

**Tom**

Now
because of you Lady
I can go

here!

there!

**Donna**

but I've imprisoned me!

**Tom**

My Laaaaady!

My Saaaaaviour!

My Mistreeeeeessssss . . .

I can go . . .

**Donna**

Even when men've . . . (*died*)
Even when they've become . . . (*putrid ectoplasm*)

**Tom**

. . . here . . .

**Donna**

Even . . . (*hideously disfigured*)

**Tom**

. . . there!

**Donna**

they still think you're there just to listen
to them . . .

**Tom**

Outside. What is that?
What is the rrrrrrrrr sound constant in the air? /
Thinges exploding sometimes. / What is that?
Lot of shininess in / . . . this

```
This      is strange. /
This      is strange.
Light.      But how?
This.      What?
```

*Donna, losing interest, flicks through a magazine as she answers.*

**Donna**
Traffic.
Fireworks.
Glass.
Plastic.
'Elle Decoration.'
Silk Cut King Size.

**Tom**
How look I now?

**Donna** (*texting on her mobile*)
Terrible.

**Tom**
I was handsome of face!!!!

**Donna**
Yeah . . . ?

**Tom**
Time!

*She goes for her mobile, dials.*

**Donna**
Kulvinder . . . give us a bell
you fancy hooking up doing
something . . . 'kay?

*She re-dials.*

**Tom**
What time is it?

**Donna**

It's Day 4983 in the Big Brother House . . .
eleven fifty-six p.m.
Keith? . . . Fancy a video and Indian? Text me.

**Tom**

I'm still in the room
but my body feels like nothing!
What does this mean?

Lovely Lady?

**Donna** (*to Tom*)

I'm guessing 'Limbo'
You should ring Derek Acorah.

**Tom**

I think I smell!

*She re-dials.*

**Donna**

You do. Big time.

*On mobile.*

Marcia?
If you fancy going late power-walking . . .
call me.

*To audience.*

Stuck indoors no date Saturday night.
Unlucky.
Stuck indoors no date Saturday-night stalker.
Problem now this . . . ????
It's taking unlucky to the next level isn't it???

**Tom**

Oh Tom!
Oh poor poor Tom!

**Donna**
   Oh Donna!
   Oh poor poor Donna!!!

*Theresa's landline rings. Two rings, then a message.*

**Theresa** (*on phone*)
   Donna! Don't pick this up!
   Just listen and do exactly what I tell you!
   Look at your text messages!
   Then get out of my flat!
   Out     Of     My     Flat!
   Hide Somewhere!
   Anywhere!
   But Hide!
   Oh God, Donna . . .
   He's coming!!!
   He's Coming To Get Me!!!
   He's . . .
   Rod!!!

**Rod**
   Theresa!
   What you using that for?
   Don't use that!
   You really don't want to use /

*The phone cuts off abruptly.*

**Donna**
   Theresa . . . ?

   THERESA!!!!

   *End of Act One*

86

# Act Two

## TWENTY: DECOMPOSING

**Donna**
Theresa . . . ?

THERESA!!!!

*She tries to call Theresa on the landline.*

**Tom**
What is this . . . ?

**Donna**
Phone!!!     Theresa?

Theresa?

THERESA!!!!

*No answer. She tries her mobile.*

**Tom**
What is this . . . ?

**Donna**
Mobile phone!!!

Theresa?

*No answer.*

*She accesses her texts. Reads.*

'Candle-Man has got me!
In his van bringing me back.
Must Not Repeat Not
Find You There.
Get Out     A     S     A     P

I Am his Breakfast . . .'

Theresa!!!

**Tom**
Breakfast!

Am I hungry?

*She replays the message.*

**Theresa** (*on phone*)
Donna! Don't pick this up!
Just listen and do exactly what I tell you!
Look at your text messages!
Then get out of my flat!
Out     Of     My     Flat!
Hide Somewhere!
Anywhere!
But Hide!
Oh God, Donna . . .
He's coming!!!
He's Coming To Get Me!!!
He's . . .
Rod!!!

**Rod**
Theresa!
What you using that for?
Don't use that!
You really don't want to use –

*The phone cuts off abruptly.*

**Donna**
Oh My God!

**Tom**
Shall we pray?

**Donna**
Oh My God!!!

*There is a tremendous crash. A door flies open. Rod stands there, a tyre-lever in his hand.*

**Donna**
Oh     My     God!!!!!

**Tom** (*simultaneously*)
Oh My God!!!

**Rod**
No door was too thick for him
no bolt was too strong for him
no lock was too complex of design
it was as if he had super-powers . . .

Fancy running into you . . .

**Donna**
What have you done???!!!

**Rod**
Burglar alarms security systems
CCTV nothing stopped him
the man hisself
effected entry.

**Donna**
You're     mad     as     fuck!!!

**Rod**
There's really no need for bad language.
Cup of tea be nice.

**Donna**
Where's Theresa?

**Rod**
That's my business, don't you think?

**Tom**
Does he mean us harm?
What weapon is that?

**Donna**

Where's Theresa????

**Rod**

That's for me to know . . .

*He moves about the room to . . .*

Bit of a chill in here.

Yep.

Bit of a nasty smell here.

Yep.

*Tom moves back, but Rod comes nose to nose with him, smelling . . .*

Just here.

**Tom**

Who are you?

*Rod cannot see him.*

**Rod**

What this room needs is

some central heating adjustments

and

an aromatic candle.

*He picks up the large ceramic pot-pourri container, hands it to Donna.*

**Donna**

What have you done with Theresa?

**Rod**

She's fine.

**Donna**

What?

**Rod**
> She's been taken care of.

**Tom**
> Some man threatens my Mistress
> but he doesn't listen
> I cannot make him stop . . .
> What does that mean?
>
> What Does That Mean????

**Donna**
> Taken care of . . . ????

**Rod**
> She's fine.
>
> Men
> Women
> Children
> all somehow trusted him
> even Animals
>
> She's fine. It's Sorted.

**Donna**
> What have you done?
> What have you done to Theresa?

> *She leaps upon Rod, hitting him with the ceramic pot-pourri container.*
>
> You Mad Sod You
> You mad bloody sod what have you
> done with her???

**Rod**
> Hey . . .
>
> No . . . Hey!!!!

**Tom**
> She attacks him.

I cannot!!!

What does this mean?

*The ceramic shatters. She gets the tyre-lever.*

**Donna**
You did something to my friend?

To my friend????

*She brings the tyre-lever down. He wrestles with her.*

**Rod**
You stop that no! Ouch!!!
No! . . . Don't, it hurts!!!

**Donna**
Theresa! Where's Theresa?

*She gets the lever free.*

**Rod**
That's my tyre-lever!

**Donna**
Have it then!!!!

*She brings the tyre-lever down, aiming for his head but catching his shoulder.*

**Rod**
Oya!      Oya!!!!

**Tom**
She is murdering him!

But I cannot!

What does this mean?

**Donna**
Leave us alone!!!!

This a clear enough message for you?

*She rains blows at his head, using any heavy object she finds.*

This getting through to you?

This getting through your thick skull?

Leave us alone!!!!

*She gets the pillow, cushions, smothers him. Duvet.
    Rod dies. Donna, exhausted, straddles him. Tom hovers.*

**Tom**
She's killed him.

He's dead.

(*Thinks.*) Am I dead?

*Rod is in a crumpled heap, Donna on top of him.*

Am I dead?

**Donna**
Oh . . . Theresa!

*Theresa appears in the shattered door.*

**Theresa**
Don't tell me that mad bastard
just broke down my door!!!

I said, 'I've no keys, we're going to have
to Problem-Solve.'
He said, 'Onto It. Sorted!'

I said, 'Give me a second, I'm parking the car.'

*She looks at her door.*

The mad bastard

*Looks around the flat.*

Where is he?

**Tom**

I know this lady.

Is she dead?

Am I dead?

**Theresa**

Donna!
Tell me you haven't had a bloody party!!!
Tell me bloody Kulvinder hasn't been round
with some commis chefs!

*She sees Donna on the duvet-covered mound.*

Donna?

*Following a horrible suspicion, she looks under the
duvet . . .*

Oh, kid, No . . .

*She sees how dead Rod is.*

Is he oh he isn't say he isn't please God
say he isn't is he is he oh he is!

**Donna**

Oh . . . Theresa!!!!

**Theresa**

I'm sooooo not believing this . . .

**Donna**

I'm like, 'Where's Theresa what have you
done with Theresa?' and he's like, 'She's
fine she's sorted,' and he's holding
like a tyre-lever so I'm like, 'He's topped
her he's topped Theresa.'

**Theresa**

You coulda checked, kid!
That's why God invented mobiles, Donna!

94

**Donna**

I did! Your mobile was dead!

**Theresa**

Bloody texting you, pot-herb!!!

*They look at Rod.*

I'd better call the police yeah?

And ambulance yeah?

You never know? Outside chance he's . . .
Fingers cr . . .
Hello, could you send a police car please
There's been an incident
a serious incident
yes . . . ambulance might be a good . . .
it's . . . domestic violence . . .
The perpetrator's with my yeah
and the victim yeah . . .
but there's like mitigating circumstances
we'll be wanting you to take on board . . .
No, I'm not her lawyer!

*Quite pleased about this, though.*

I just . . . yeah . . .
*Miami CSI* . . . yeah . . . it's great
oh, and I think we've got a stiff . . .
yeah
yeah
yeah
no
12b Marlborough Mansions

They're coming straight away.

*They both sit.*

95

**Tom**
Am I dead?

*Donna gets out her cigarettes.*

**Donna**
Theresa . . . D'you mind if I . . . ?

**Theresa**
Well . . . just this once!

*Both do a very pale imitation of the stereo laugh.*
*Donna lights up. Tom materialises.*

**Tom**
Am I dead???

**Donna**
Theresa . . . can you see anything . . .

*Points at Tom.*

. . . there?

**Theresa**
Yes. My Purely bloody Poppy
All over my bloody wall!
Thank you very much, Donna!

*Donna smokes gently.*

**Donna**
Nothing else?

Nothing      supernatural . . . ???

**Theresa**
How much of my bloody Baileys have you had???

**Donna**
Just me then.

Typical!

**Tom**
  My mistress!!!

**Donna**
  No!!!

**Tom**
  My Lady!!!

**Donna**
  Shhhhh!!!

**Tom**
  My Saviour!!!

**Donna**
  Just a few minutes peace!!!
  Okay . . . ???
  Just a bit of Me Time!!!
  Okay???

**Theresa**
  What?

**Donna**
  Nothing.

*Tom hovers into sitting beside the two live women.*

**Donna**
  God, Theresa . . .
  your flat's fucking freezing!!!

**Theresa**
  Well . . . Problem. End of.
  I think I'll be moving now,
  thank you very much
  don't you?

**Donna**
  Oh, Theresa.

*The three sit for a moment or two.*

**Theresa**
So . . . how was your weekend . . .
Restful?

*Both a little stereo laugh.*

**Donna**
Bloody Awful!

*Both laugh.*

Yours?

**Theresa**
The Love Tryst.
Camera.
Action.
Door of Room 506
The Viking Motel Kettering
swings open . . .

Barry's sitting on the bed
He's wearing Hilfiger top not clean
sweatpants ditto trainers ditto
his tan's too donkey-brown for Northants
I'm not impressed.

It was tempestuous in Tenerife.

in Kettering      it's crap.

Question arises . . .
if Barry's sitting on the bed looking crap . . .
who's opened the door?

**Donna**
The wife?

**Theresa**
That's your final answer?

98

You've won yourself £32,000!
The wife.

She's taken the trouble to do
the Bobbi Brown (*make-up*) . . .
the Jennifer Lopez (*hair*) . . .
the Max Mara . . .

I'm impressed.

She says
'Welcome to Kettering I'm Norma, Barry's wife.
We've a few things to sort out.
Tea? Coffee? Something Stronger?
There's no room service we'll
send Barry we don't need him for this.'
As Rod said . . .
she behaved with quiet dignity
her heart had been broken by a lesser human
her eyes looked bruised by life.

**Donna**
Rod?
You mean . . .
this Rod . . . ?
my Rod?

**Theresa**
We'll get to whose Rod in a minute . . .
Norma's like, 'You should know
I'm not going to give him up . . .'
I'm like, 'I understand,' she says, 'Do you stuff
you could have him tomorrow but I've three kids
need trainers and a home computer to pay for.'
I said, 'He wants to be with me,'
she said, 'He wanted to be with Marie-Berte
from Oslo but if I can persuade
her against it with her lack of a command
of the English Language I can persuade you

have you ever seen him without his tan
you'll get over him.'

I liked her.

**Donna**

And you're always fair.

**Theresa**

Rod's like . . . 'You're a woman of principle.
With a great big heart.'

**Donna**

My Rod?
This Rod?

**Theresa**

We'll get to it . . .
I'm like, 'You know what? He's yours.'
I leave.
I meet Barry on the stairs.
I'm like, 'I'll never forget you Barry
but it's so over.'
He's like, 'I'll never forget you . . .'
and I swear he's going to call me . . .
but, you know what? I say, 'You know
what, Barry, don't call me.'
I'd have been out of there without a
backward glance
but there's a big palaver going on in 509.

*She looks down quite fondly at Rod.*

You followed the wrong person into
the wrong room, didn't you, Mr Surveillance?

There's a shit-scared transvestite from
Retford washing out his pantyhose right now . . .
(*To Donna.*) Your bloody car wouldn't start.
Flat bloody battery.

Twat.
Now Mission Impossible has joined me.
I'm like . . .
'I need a lift.'
He's like, 'Your every wish is my command.'
I'm like, 'Fetch me weekend case from 507.'
He's like, 'Your every wish is my command' . . .
I said, 'Is this your van open the passenger door?'
He's like,
'Let me take you away from all this.'
I said, 'I've had Major Heartbreak
back there and I need to come to terms with it
and move on . . .
you can talk to me . . .
take me mind off it all.'
Do you know how to make candles, Donna?

**Donna**

Oh God candles.

*She lights another cigarette. Tom lets out a slight
moan.*

Shhhh!

Not you, Tree . . .

**Theresa**

He's like, 'Can I action any of your demands?'
I'm like, 'Got any travel sweets?'
He's like, 'I'm very careful what I put in my body.'
I said, 'I can see that.'
He's like, 'I could pull into a Little Chef your
every wish is my command,' and he's buying me
the All-Day-Big-Breakfast and I mention
the problems I'm having with the central heating
and he's like, 'Central heating? That's my department'
and 'Banishing unwanted odours? That's my
department!!!'

So I think, 'Strike while the iron's hot
bring him back here!!!'
You see . . . any man . . .
manage them . . . refuse to be a victim . . .
boss them . . .
Sorted!!!

**Donna**
Oh Theresa . . .
you don't wanna Go There!

**Theresa**
Well . . .

*Indicates Rod's bleeding body.*

Donna . . . end of.

*Takes something out of her pocket.*

And I think this is going to stop at
'the prototype'.

*She is holding a candle in the shape of two ample breasts.*

Should we light it?

Sort of . . . mark of respect?

*Theresa holds out the breasts. Donna lights both nipples with her lighter.*

**Tom**
I'm dead. Aren't I?

He's dead. Isn't he?

Women. Frightening, aren't you?

*Both women shudder in stereo.*

**Donna**
So.

Police be here soon.

**Theresa**
  Yeah.

  I'm guessing two totally fit objects
  mine      blonde hair piercing blue eyes

**Donna**
  mine      dark hair good cut
  but      short

**Theresa**
  well . . . Old Bill

**Donna**
  and gentle but strong eyes

**Theresa**
  and they're both good men

**Donna**
  they're policemen, Theresa.
  And they fall in love with us.

**Theresa**
  And they look after us

  And they're not married.

  *A sound of police sirens.*

**Donna**
  Oo!

**Theresa**
  You're gonna be famous, kid.
  Your self-defence slaughter.
  I'm gonna be famous. I lent my flat to a friend.
  I came back to
  a Bloodbath.

**Donna**
  We'll be Celebrities.

**Theresa**
We'll have made it, twat.

**Donna**
I'm just going to do my affirmations, yeah? For Good
Luck . . .

**Theresa**
Alright, kid.

**Donna**
I will never ever
accept anything less than the love
I deserve . . .

*She says this three times. Theresa joins in on three.*

**Both**
I will never ever accept anything
less than the love I deserve . . .

**Donna**
It's an affirmation, Theresa,
you got to do it three times
for it to work . . .

**Theresa**
I will never ever
accept anything less than the love
I deserve . . .

*Donna coaches and corrects.*

**Donna**
. . . anything less
love . . .
I deserve

*On the third, Tom joins in.*

**Donna**
One more time for luck?

*The three repeat the affirmation . . .*

**All Three**
I will never ever
accept anything less than
The love I deserve . . .

*. . . as the doorbell rings. Loud knock at the door.*
*Rod suddenly flickers into ghostly being, hovering*
*over his own duvet-strewn corpse.*

**Rod**
I will never ever
Accept anything less than
The love I deserve . . .

*Curtain.*